Unveiling the Enigmatic Beauty of Spain.

OVIEDO, SPAIN TRAVEL GUIDE 2024

ETHAN BRISBANE

TABLE OF CONTENTS

CHAPTER I

INTRODUCTION

I was enthralled with Oviedo's ageless charm as I stood in the centre of the city, surrounded by buildings that date back hundreds of years and the soft murmur of commerce. The smell of freshly made pastries filled the air and the cobblestone streets murmured stories of times gone by, enticing me to explore more. This charming city is tucked away in the verdant Asturian countryside of Spain and offers a wealth of adventures just waiting to be explored.

I cordially invite you to tour with me through Oviedo with this travel guide, a city where creativity blends with history and tradition meets modernity. Oviedo offers a complex tapestry of sights, sounds, and flavours that will captivate you, whether you're an experienced tourist looking for new experiences or a curious explorer ready to find hidden jewels.

But you would wonder, why Oviedo? Why would you want to travel to this charming city in 2024? Its dynamic energy and steadfast spirit, in addition to its stunning beauty, hold the key to its explanation. Oviedo is an experience—a chance to fully immerse oneself in a culture that embraces life, love, and the small pleasures of existence—rather than merely a place to visit.

Come along with me as we explore the historical sites, indulge in the local cuisine, and learn about the rich cultural legacy of Oviedo. Every part of Oviedo, from the imposing San Salvador Cathedral to the busy Old Town streets, has a memory and a tale waiting to be discovered.

1.1 An overview of Oviedo

Tucked away in the lush Asturian countryside, Oviedo is a vibrant, historically rich city. Its origins are rooted in the Middle Ages, and its rich history is evident everywhere you look. Oviedo radiates an air of timeless grandeur, from the antique Romanesque churches that dot the skyline to the majestic Gothic architecture of the Cathedral of San Salvador.

However, Oviedo is a bustling city that teems with life and vitality, not merely a living museum of the past. While the contemporary avenues are filled with bustling cafes, stylish boutiques, and vibrant markets, the Old Town's cobblestone alleyways are alive with the laughter and chatter of both locals and visitors. Oviedo offers something for everyone, whether you're an outdoor explorer, foodie, history lover, or art aficionado.

1.2 Why Visit Oviedo in 2024

Now, you might be asking yourself, why should I plan to visit Oviedo in 2024? The plethora of adventures that await you and the city's undeniable charm hold the answer. Permit me to describe to you what Oviedo has in store for you this coming year:

- **Cultural Celebrations:** Oviedo is expected to come alive in 2024 with a wide range of festivals and events. There are plenty of opportunities to get immersed in the local way of life, such as the lively Fiesta de San Mateo, which honours the city's patron saint with music, dance, and traditional processions, and the International Film Festival of Gijón, which offers film enthusiasts a wide range of avant-garde films.

- **Gastronomic Delights:** Get ready for an unparalleled gastronomic experience. Oviedo is well known for its delicious Asturian food, which includes a variety of tantalising delicacies including cachopo, an opulent meal laden with meat, and of course, sidra, a classic Asturian cider. Fabuada asturiana is a robust bean stew. Dining in Oviedo is an adventure in and of itself, with a plethora of quaint cider houses, inviting pubs, and Michelin-starred restaurants to pick from.

- **Outdoor Adventures:** Oviedo is a true paradise for those who enjoy the outdoors and the natural world. The city, which is surrounded by beautiful mountains and rich vegetation, has an abundance of outdoor activities suitable for all interests and skill levels. There are plenty of opportunities to reconnect with nature and revitalise your spirit, whether you're biking along the gorgeous Senda del Oso trail, trekking through the breathtaking Picos de Europa National Park, or just taking a stroll through the serene parks and gardens that dot the metropolis.

- Oviedo boasts an enormous collection of magnificent artwork and architectural marvels. There's no lack of places to indulge your creative tastes, from the famous Eduardo Chillida sculptures that line the city's plazas to the cutting-edge shows at the Centro de Arte Rupestre de Tito Bustillo. Now is a great time to discover Oviedo's rich cultural legacy, as numerous historic buildings and sites have been revitalised by recent restoration initiatives.

To sum up, Oviedo is calling you in with open arms to explore its mysteries, taste its delicacies, and make lifelong memories. Why then wait? Prepare for an incredible journey into the heart of Oviedo—a city where the past and present collide and where there is always a new adventure waiting to be discovered—by packing your bags, purchasing your ticket, and travelling with me.

CHAPTER II

GETTING STARTED

Essential Information, Travel Tips, and Safety Precautions

Greetings from Oviedo, the starting point of the captivating Asturian region of Spain! As your experienced tour guide, I'm here to make sure your trip to Oviedo goes as smoothly and pleasurably as possible by giving you useful travel advice, vital information, and crucial safety instructions.

2.1 Essential Information:

- **Location:** Oviedo is in the autonomous community of Asturias, in the northern region of Spain. It is encircled by the breathtaking Cantabrian Mountains and is tucked away in a verdant landscape.
- **Language:** Spanish is the official language used in Oviedo and all of Spain. Even though a lot of people in the area could know a little bit of English, it's always beneficial to pick up a few fundamental Spanish words to improve your trip and interact with people more efficiently.

- **Currency:** The Euro (€) is the currency used in Oviedo and the rest of Spain. For modest transactions, you should have extra cash on hand because not all businesses, particularly in more remote locations, may take credit or debit cards.
- Oviedo is in the Central European Time (CET) zone, which is UTC+1 during standard time and UTC+2 during summer daylight saving time.
- Oviedo experiences pleasant temperatures and consistent rains all year round due to its temperate marine environment. Summers are pleasant and mild, with average highs of 20–25°C (68–77°F), and winters are chilly and wet, with highs of 8–12°C (46–54°F). Before your vacation, it's a good idea to check the weather forecast and make appropriate packing decisions.

2.2 Travel Advice:

- **Plan Ahead:** Spend some time researching and creating your itinerary before leaving for Oviedo. Decide which must-see sights, events, and activities you just must not miss. To minimise disappointment, think about booking in advance for popular excursions and dining establishments.
- **Pack Light:** Because Oviedo has small, cobblestone streets and is a walkable city, it's essential to bring light

clothing and wear comfortable walking shoes. Because the weather can change quickly, especially in the highlands, make sure you bring layers of clothes and a waterproof jacket.

- **Stay Connected:** While many parks and plazas in Oviedo provide free Wi-Fi, it's a good idea to purchase a local SIM card or set up an international roaming plan on your phone to keep connected while travelling. When exploring the city, having access to communication tools, translation applications, and maps can be quite helpful.

- **Taste the Local Food:** Savouring the mouthwatering Asturian cuisine is one of the main attractions of Oviedo. Enjoy regional specialties including sidra (Asturian cider), cachopo (fried and breaded beef or pork filled with cheese and ham), and fabada asturiana (bean stew). For a genuine gastronomic experience, don't be scared to stray from the usual route and visit little, family-run eateries.

- Respect Local Customs: Keep in mind to show respect for the customs and traditions of Oviedo as you explore the city. When visiting places of worship like churches and cathedrals, dress modestly and always get permission before taking pictures of people or their property. Additionally, since service fees are typically included in the bill, tipping is not common in Spain.

2.3 Safety Precautions:

- **Stay Vigilant:** Although Oviedo is a generally safe place for tourists to visit, it's still advisable to be alert and aware of your surroundings, particularly in crowded tourist areas or late at night. Always keep your possessions safe, and refrain from flaunting expensive electronics or jewellery.

- **Use Licensed Transportation:** Be careful to use trustworthy and licensed companies while taking public transportation or booking taxis in Oviedo. Unlicensed or unofficial taxis should not be accepted for rides since they might not follow safety rules or fare requirements.

- **Stay Informed:** Throughout your visit to Oviedo, keep yourself updated on any local safety advisories, weather alerts, or emergency protocols. In the event of an emergency, be familiar with the closest hospitals or medical facilities and have emergency contact numbers on hand, such as the local police's number (112) and the medical services' number (061).

- Oviedo is renowned for its vibrant nightlife, but it's crucial to use caution when drinking and to be aware of your boundaries. To reduce the chance of drink spiking or theft, pace your alcohol use and never leave your drink unattended.

- **Observe COVID-19 Guidelines:** To protect yourself and others during the ongoing COVID-19 pandemic, you must abide by local health and safety regulations. This can entail using a face mask in indoor public areas, engaging in social distancing, and abiding by any particular rules or guidelines put in place by regional authorities.

You may travel to Oviedo with confidence if you heed this crucial advice and take the necessary safety measures, as you'll be well-equipped to enjoy yourself to the fullest while remaining secure. Thus, gather your belongings, embark on your journey, and get ready to be mesmerised by Oviedo's allure and the surrounding Asturian landscape.

CHAPTER III

FREQUENTLY ASKED QUESTIONS

Welcome to our travel guide's section on frequently asked questions (FAQ) about Oviedo! I'm here to give you all the information you need to organise your trip to this quaint city in northern Spain as your amiable and competent tour guide. Now let's explore some of the most often asked questions visitors have about Oviedo.

Q1. Which season is ideal for travelling to Oviedo?

The ideal time to visit Oviedo will depend on your interests and preferences. The various seasons and their offerings are broken down as follows:

- **Spring (March to May):** Oviedo's springtime is a pleasant season, with comfortable temperatures between 10 and 20°C (50 and 68°F). Explore the parks, gardens, and outdoor cafes at this charming time of year when the city comes alive with blossoming flowers. In addition, you'll be spared the throngs of people that descend on Oviedo in the height of summer.

- **Summer (June to August):** With pleasant average temperatures of 20–25°C (68–77°F), summer is Oviedo's busiest travel period. This is the ideal time of year to engage in outdoor pursuits like cycling and hiking as well as visiting the city's cultural attractions. Just be ready for more people and more expensive pricing, particularly in well-known tourist destinations.

- **Autumn (September to November):** With temperatures starting to drop to between 10 and 20°C (50 and 68°F), autumn is still a great season to visit Oviedo. Autumnal hues of orange and gold adorn the landscape, providing a picturesque setting for discovering the city's parks and the neighbouring rural areas. You'll also be able to take part in regional food events and harvest festivals.

- **Winter (December to February):** Oviedo experiences a reasonably warm winter, with average highs of 5 to 10°C (41 to 50°F). This is still a terrific time to visit if you want to take in the Christmas spirit of the city, even though the weather may be a little colder. It's also easier to explore the city's attractions at your own pace because there are fewer people and cheaper pricing.

The ideal time to travel to Oviedo ultimately depends on your interests and the things you want to see and do there. Oviedo has lots to offer all year round, whether you're looking for warm days for outdoor activities or cosy evenings by the fire in a classic Asturian cider house.

Q2. Which Oviedo attractions are a must-see?

Oviedo has a lot to offer visitors, including historical sites, cultural centres, and breathtaking natural formations. During your vacation, you won't want to miss these must-see attractions:

- **Cathedral of San Salvador:** One of Oviedo's most recognizable buildings is this magnificent Gothic cathedral, which dates to the eighth century. Explore its fascinating history and theological significance while admiring its magnificent architecture, which includes the beautifully carved stone facade and high bell tower.

- **Old Town (Casco Antiguo):** Explore Oviedo's enchanting Old Town, which is home to a plethora of historic structures, quaint squares, and authentic Asturian cider houses, as you meander through its winding cobblestone streets. Don't miss the Plaza del Fontán, a lively market square with cafes and stores surrounding it, and the Plaza de la Catedral, which is the location of the cathedral and other notable buildings.

- **Campoamor Theater:** Enter the sophisticated Campoamor Theater, Oviedo's top performing arts facility, and be astounded by its lavish furnishings and intricate workmanship. Experience the charm of this historic theatre, which has played host to world-class performers and cultural events since its inception in 1892. Take a guided tour or see a live performance.

- Explore the pre-Romanesque churches of Asturia, San Miguel de Lillo, and Santa María del Naranco, which are located outside the city centre and are both recognized as UNESCO World Heritage Sites. Admire their geometric designs, dexterous carvings, and breathtaking views of the mountains while discovering their importance as early Middle Ages architectural masterpieces.

- **Monte Naranco:** This picturesque mountain range, which is situated just outside of Oviedo, is a great place to get away from the bustle of the city and reconnect with nature. For sweeping views of the city and the surrounding countryside, hike or drive to the summit. While there, take in the famous Naranco structures, such as the Santa María del Naranco and San Miguel de Lillo churches from the ninth century.

These are but a handful of the numerous attractions in Oviedo that are waiting for you. This fascinating city offers a plethora of sights and activities for individuals with diverse interests, including history, culture, art, and nature.

Q3. How is the year-round weather in Oviedo?

Oviedo experiences year-round warm temperatures and light rainfall due to its temperate oceanic environment. An outline of the typical weather trends in Oviedo is shown below:

- **Spring:** Daytime highs in Oviedo range from 10 to 20°C (50 to 68°F), bringing with them moderate temperatures and blossoming flowers. But keep in mind that springtime can also bring sporadic downpours, so don't forget to carry an umbrella and waterproof clothing.
- **Summer:** Oviedo experiences mild, pleasant summers with average temperatures between 20 and 25°C (68 and 77°F). Summertime brings less rain, but it can also mean higher humidity, particularly in July and August. If you plan to spend any time outside, remember to apply sunscreen and drink plenty of water.
- **Autumn:** Oviedo experiences milder temperatures throughout this season, with highs between 10 and 20°C (50 and 68°F), and colourful leaves. Autumn brings more rain, especially in October and November. Plan and pack appropriately for the weather by packing rain gear and shoes.
- **Winter:** Oviedo experiences comparatively moderate winters, with typical highs of 5–10°C (41–50°F). Although there isn't much snow in the city itself, snow-capped mountains are frequently seen in the

surrounding countryside. To be warm and comfortable throughout the chilly months, make sure to layer your clothes.

Oviedo has a generally moderate climate all year round, which makes it a great place to visit for sightseeing and outdoor adventure in any season. Just make sure to check the weather prediction ahead of time and pack appropriately to guarantee a relaxing and pleasurable trip.

Q4. Which kind of transportation is available in Oviedo?

Oviedo has a range of transportation choices to facilitate your exploration of the city and its environs. The following are some of the easiest ways to move around:

- **Walking:** One of the greatest ways to see Oviedo's historic sites, quaint neighbourhoods, and exciting cultural activities is on foot, as the city's small downtown is quite walkable. Put on your walking shoes and go exploring Oviedo's splendour at your speed.

- **Public Transportation:** Oviedo's bus and tram systems, which link the city centre to surrounding towns and neighbourhoods, are dependable and reasonably priced. Routes and schedules are available online, at bus stops and tram stations, and vending machines and authorised stores sell single tickets and multi-ride passes.

- **Taxi:** Taxis are widely available in Oviedo and may be scheduled ahead of time via a taxi app or by hailing one on the street. Taxis are an easy way to go for short distances or to places that are not accessible by public transit; the city authority sets the price for these services.

- **Car Rental:** Several car rental companies are situated in Oviedo. If you would rather have the freedom to drive your automobile, you can rent a car from them. You can travel at your speed through the surrounding countryside and sights if you have a car, but keep in mind that parking in the city centre might be pricey and scarce.

- **Bicycle:** Those who wish to explore Oviedo on two wheels can rent bikes from the city, which has designated bike lanes. Using a public bike-sharing program or renting a bike from one of the many rental shops is a terrific way to see the sights while being environmentally conscious and active.

These are but a handful of Oviedo's transportation choices. There are many easy methods to get around and see everything that this lovely city has to offer, whether you'd rather walk, utilise public transportation, rent a car, or ride a bike.

To sum up, Oviedo is a fascinating place that has something to offer everyone, regardless of their interests in nature, history, culture, or food. You can make the most of your time in Oviedo and make memories that will last a lifetime by scheduling your visit during the best time of year, seeing the city's must-see attractions, keeping up with the weather, and taking advantage of the many available transportation options. I hope your travels are safe and that I get to see you in Oviedo soon!

CHAPTER IV

UPDATED 2024 INFORMATION

Welcome to Oviedo, where innovation and tradition converge, and there's always something new to discover! This section will cover the most recent advancements in Oviedo, such as brand-new attractions, fascinating occasions, and adjustments to the city's culinary and entertainment offerings.

4.1 New Developments in Oviedo

Oviedo is a city that is always changing, with new projects and upgrades boosting the experience for visitors every year. The following are some recent advancements that you might anticipate in 2024:

- **Urban Renewal Initiatives:** To enhance infrastructure and revitalise its historic centre, Oviedo has launched several urban renewal initiatives. This includes restoring historic buildings, pedestrianising roadways, and renovating public areas to make the area more hospitable and conducive to pedestrian traffic for both locals and tourists.

- **Museums & Cultural Institutions:** Oviedo now has several brand-new museums and cultural institutions that provide tourists the chance to delve into the deep history and rich cultural legacy of the city. There is something to enjoy for everyone, from interactive museum exhibitions to galleries of contemporary art.

- **Parks and Green Areas:** Oviedo is well-known for its profusion of parks and gardens as well as its rich vegetation. To further highlight the city's natural beauty, additional green areas have been developed. These consist of beautifully designed gardens, picturesque vantage spots, and outdoor leisure spaces for guests to unwind in.

- Restaurants, cafes, and shops are popping up throughout Oviedo, contributing to the city's ever-evolving dining and shopping culture. There are plenty of options for those who enjoy both food and shopping, from hip restaurants offering cutting-edge cuisine to artisanal stores selling regional handicrafts.

- **Hubs for Technology and Innovation:** Oviedo is rapidly becoming known as a centre for technology and innovation, with the emergence of new businesses, coworking spaces, and incubators fostering entrepreneurship and economic expansion. For further information about the city's thriving startup ecosystem, tech-savvy visitors can visit innovation centres and go to networking events.

4.2 2024's Events and Festivals

Oviedo is renowned for its exciting festivals and thriving cultural scene, and 2024 looks to be no different. Here are a few events and festivals in Oviedo that you shouldn't miss this year:

- **Fiesta de San Mateo:** This yearly celebration honours San Mateo, the city's patron saint, and features music, dance, parades, and traditional Asturian food to highlight Oviedo's rich cultural past. During the week-long celebrations, attendees can take in street acts, craft markets, and religious processions.
- **International Film Festival of Gijón:** This well-known film festival draws filmmakers, business people, and cinema lovers from all over the world, although officially taking place in the nearby city of Gijón. Cinephiles can find new talent and masterpieces in film during screenings, workshops, and networking activities held throughout the city.
- Asturias' autumnal season is known as "cider season," and Oviedo comes alive with festivities and events centred around cider. There are plenty of opportunities to enjoy Asturian cider culture in Oviedo, ranging from cider tastings and apple-picking excursions to traditional cider-pouring competitions.
- **Christmas Markets:** Oviedo becomes a winter wonderland as the holidays draw near, with jolly Christmas markets springing up throughout the city.

Aside from live music, entertainment, and seasonal snacks, guests can peruse booths offering homemade gifts, festive décor, and regional specialties.

- **Asturias Day:** Held on September 8th, this regional celebration honours the historic Battle of Covadonga, which signalled the start of Spain's Reconquista. Visitors get a rare chance to experience Asturian pride and heritage through traditional ceremonies, cultural performances, and culinary activities throughout the festivities.

These are only a handful of the numerous celebrations and activities that Oviedo has in store for you in 2024. Make sure to keep an eye out for upcoming events and noteworthy occasions all year long by consulting the local event calendar.

4.3   Changes   in   Dining   and Entertainment Scene

With new eateries, cafes, bars, and entertainment venues coming up to suit the varied preferences of both locals and tourists, Oviedo's dining and entertainment scene is always changing. The following are some recent developments and shifts that Oviedo's dining and entertainment scenes should witness by 2024:

- **Gastronomic Innovation:** Chefs in Oviedo are experimenting with novel ingredients, cooking methods, and flavour combinations, pushing the envelope in the culinary arts. Diners may anticipate international influences from all around the world combined with traditional Asturian dishes and contemporary twists.

- **Farm-to-Table Dining:** To highlight the finest of Asturian cuisine, several restaurants and cafes in Oviedo are collaborating with regional farmers, producers, and craftsmen to source products locally and sustainably. Oviedo is a paradise for foodies who value quality and authenticity, with everything from organic markets selling fresh vegetables and artisanal products to farm-to-table restaurants providing seasonal meals.

- **Craft Cocktails & Mixology:** Oviedo has been swept up by the craft cocktail revolution, where mixologists are creating inventive concoctions with premium spirits, homemade syrups, and fresh herbs and botanicals. At hip bars and lounges all across the city, guests may enjoy inventive concoctions influenced by Asturian flavours and customs as well as traditional cocktails with a contemporary spin.

- **Live Music and Entertainment:** Oviedo is home to a strong live music scene that features a wide range of talent from local musicians to international bands at theatres and performance places. Whatever your musical tastes—electronic, jazz, flamenco, rock, or otherwise—Oviedo offers a wide range of live entertainment and cultural events.

- **Social and Cultural Hubs:** To promote creativity and collaboration and to unite the city's thriving population of artists, creatives, and culture enthusiasts, new social and cultural hubs are springing up throughout Oviedo. These hubs, which range from community centres and cultural groups to coworking spaces and art galleries, provide a place for individuals to meet, communicate, and exchange ideas.

These are only a handful of the most recent advancements and fashions influencing Oviedo's culinary and entertainment landscape in 2024. Whatever your interests—foodies, music aficionados, art enthusiasts, or just curious to check out the local way of life—Oviedo offers something to offer everyone. Come experience the city's mouthwatering cuisine, fascinating cultural offerings, and exciting nightlife to see why Oviedo is a place that has it all.

CHAPTER V

EXPLORING OVIEDO

An Adventure Through Nature, Art, and History

Welcome to Oviedo, where each historic structure and cobblestone street narrates a tale from ages gone by. We'll go around the city's colourful art scene, rich history, and stunning natural settings in this portion. Oviedo provides a multitude of experiences just waiting to be discovered, from parks and gardens to museums and galleries to historic monuments and landmarks.

5.1 Historical Sites and Landmarks

- **Cathedral of San Salvador:** The striking Cathedral of San Salvador, which stands as a tribute to the city's rich religious legacy, is where our

adventure starts in the centre of Oviedo. This imposing Gothic cathedral, which dates to the eighth century, is a work of mediaeval architectural art with its elaborate chapels, tall spires, and detailed stone carvings. Enter to see its magnificent interior, which includes the Tomb of King Alfonso II, the Altar of the Holy Savior, and the Camara Santa, a UNESCO World Heritage Site that is home to priceless relics and antiques.

- **Old Town (Casco Antiguo):** We will come across a wealth of old buildings, secret courtyards, and lovely plazas as we meander through the quaint Old Town of Oviedo. The Plaza  del Fontán, a vibrant market square with vibrant facades and busy cafes surrounding it, and the Plaza de la Catedral, which is home to the cathedral and other notable buildings, are two of the city's highlights. Every corner of the area offers a fresh surprise, so make sure to explore the meandering and mediaeval passageways.

- Two of the most famous pre-Romanesque churches in Oviedo are San Miguel de Lillo and Santa María del Naranco, and they are both only a short drive from the city centre. These historic churches, which are located atop the picturesque Monte Naranco mountainside, were built in the ninth century and are well-known for their superb architecture and stunning views of the surrounding mountains. Travel back in time to the early Middle Ages and be amazed by the geometric patterns, artistic embellishments, and well-carved stone façade.

- **Campoamor Theater:** A visit to the sophisticated Campoamor Theater, a cultural icon that has been delighting audiences since 1892, would  conclude our exploration of Oviedo's past. Enter to see its lavish interior design, which includes velvet drapes, gilded balconies, and elaborate chandeliers, and discover its rich past as Asturias's top performing arts location. To truly feel the beauty of this ancient theatre, take a guided tour or see a live play.

- **University of Oviedo:** If we continue our exploration, we'll come upon the famed University of Oviedo, which was established in 1608 and is located in a stunning neoclassical structure that was formerly a monastery.

Admire its enormous library, which holds a sizable collection of rare volumes and manuscripts, as well as its stately exterior and large courtyards. Wander about the campus to experience the ethos of scholarly distinction and inquisitiveness that has characterised Oviedo for generations.

5.2 Galleries and Museums

- The Asturias Archaeological Museum (Museo Arqueológico de Asturias) is the next stop on our tour of Oviedo's cultural history. Its displays and relics provide  an enlightening look into the area's prehistoric past. The museum's collections, which include everything from Roman relics and prehistoric implements to mediaeval jewels and Asturian folklore, offer insightful perspectives into the history, customs, and culture of Asturias.

- Art fans will love the Museum of Fine Arts of Asturias (Museo de Bellas Artes de Asturias), which is home to an extraordinary collection of European and Spanish art from the Middle Ages to the present. Admire the creations of regional Asturian painters and sculptors as well as famous artists like El Greco, Goya, and Picasso. Throughout the year, various activities and rotating exhibitions enrich the museum's permanent collection.

- Welcome to the Asturias Railway Museum (Museo del Ferrocarril de Asturias)! Explore vintage locomotives, carriages, and railway artefacts at the Asturias Railway  Museum and take a trip back in time to the heyday of train transport. Discover the history of the Asturian railway, from its beginnings in the 1800s to its current function as a means of moving people and products around the area. Don't pass up the chance to board a restored steam train and feel the excitement of bygone eras of railroad travel.

- **Laboral Ciudad de la Cultura:** Situated a short distance from Oviedo, this expansive cultural complex is built in an old industrial structure that was formerly utilised as a vocational school. These days, a wide variety of cultural institutions, such as art galleries, performance venues, and educational facilities, call it home. Attend live music performances, browse contemporary art exhibits, and take part in innovative and creative workshops and events are all available to visitors.

- Located in the neighbouring city of Avilés, a short drive from Oviedo, is a state-of-the-art cultural facility named Centro Niemeyer in honour of the well-known Brazilian architect Oscar Niemeyer. The centre, which was created by Niemeyer himself, is a must-visit location for fans of art and architecture due to its spectacular architecture and cutting-edge design. Experience its exhibition areas, outdoor sculptures, and cultural events to fully immerse yourself in the inventive spirit that characterises this singular cultural complex.

5.3 Gardens and Parks

- San Francisco Park is a serene haven of greenery and calm that is tucked away in the centre of Oviedo's Old Town. Take a stroll through its verdant gardens, marvel at the vibrant flowers and aromatic herbs, and take in the views of the nearby historic structures and sites. San Francisco Park offers serene areas, decorative fountains, and shaded walkways that make it the ideal location to get away from the bustle of the city and reconnect with nature.
- **Campo de San Francisco:** The biggest and most well-known park in Oviedo is located as we continue to explore the city. This vast urban park, which covers more than 90 acres, provides a wide range of recreational

activities, such as birdwatching, outdoor concerts, and
running and
picnicking.

Discover
hidden
treasures like
the botanical
garden and
the
playgrounds for kids strewn throughout the park as you
walk through its picturesque ponds, lush woods, and
winding pathways.

- **El Bosque de la Zoreda:** Just outside of Oviedo, El
Bosque de la Zoreda is a lush forest that provides miles of
hiking routes, picturesque overlooks, and opportunities
to spot wildlife for those seeking a more immersive
outdoor experience. Keep a look out for local wildlife like
deer, wild boar, and foxes as you meander through thick
forests of oak, beech, and chestnut trees. Bring a picnic
lunch and explore this fascinating natural beauty all day
long.

- **Parque de Invierno:** As the name implies, Parque de
Invierno, also known as Winter Park, is a well-liked
outdoor entertainment area that welcomes guests of all
ages and offers a variety of amenities and activities. Apart
from its verdant areas and charming pathways, the park
offers recreational amenities, sports courts, and cultural

sites including the Archaeological Museum and Botanical Garden. Everyone may find something to enjoy at Parque de Invierno, whether they want to explore, work out, or just unwind.

- La Providencia Park is a charming riverbank park with breathtaking views of the surrounding countryside and mountains. It is tucked away on the banks of the Nalón River in the nearby town of Siero. Enjoy a picnic on the verdant riverfront, take a stroll by the river, or hire a paddleboat to explore the peaceful Nalón waters. La Providencia Park is the ideal location for a leisurely day of outdoor exploration and relaxation because of its picturesque beauty and tranquil ambiance.

We hope you have a greater understanding of Oviedo's rich cultural heritage, creative legacy, and natural beauty as we come to the end of our tour around the city's historical sites, museums, galleries, parks, and gardens. Oviedo has a wealth of activities waiting to be discovered, whether you're an adventure-seeking nature lover, art enthusiast, or history buff. Come experience the charm of Oviedo, where every corner offers a fresh adventure and every minute is a voyage of discovery, and discover the city's hidden gems and undiscovered tales.

CHAPTER VI

ITINERARY

Welcome to Oviedo, a city rich in culture, history, and scenic beauty around every corner. I'll lay out a thorough schedule in this section to make the most of your visit to this fascinating city. Oviedo has something to offer everyone, including outdoor excursions in the surrounding countryside, cultural immersion, and visiting the Old Town's cobblestone alleyways. Now let's look at our three-day schedule:

Day 1: Discovering Old Town

Morning:

- In Oviedo's Old Town, begin your day with a leisurely breakfast at one of the quaint eateries. Enjoy classic Asturian dishes like chocolate-covered churros or a filling tortilla española, served with a hot cup of café with leche.
- Take a guided walking tour of Old Town after breakfast to learn about its historical sites and undiscovered gems. Wander around the Plaza del Fontán, where a thriving marketplace offers locally produced goods, flowers, and fresh fruit, and take in the stunning grandeur of the San Salvador Cathedral.

- Follow the winding cobblestone streets as you explore them, pausing to take in the vibrant facades, elaborate churches, and charming squares that are what make Old Town so charming. Don't pass up the chance to see the famous Campoamor Theater and the mediaeval University of Oviedo, two architectural marvels that provide insight into the rich cultural legacy of the city.

In the afternoon:
- Visit a traditional Asturian cider house (sidrería) for lunch to enjoy the region's delicious food and well-known cider. Savour foods like empanadas (savoury pastries filled with meat or shellfish), cachopo (breaded and fried beef or pig loaded with cheese and ham), and fabada asturiana (bean stew).
- Explore the Museum of Fine Arts of Asturias, which has an amazing collection of Spanish and European art from the Middle Ages to the present, in the afternoon after lunch. Admire the creations of regional Asturian painters and sculptors as well as famous artists like El Greco, Goya, and Picasso.
- Take a stroll through San Francisco Park, an oasis of greenery and calm in the middle of Old Town, as the afternoon comes to an end. Before supper, unwind on a seat near the pond, feed the ducks, and take in the tranquil surroundings.

Evening:

- Visit one of Old Town's many eateries or taverns for dinner to savour authentic Asturian food in a warm, welcoming atmosphere. Savour regional delicacies like Asturian meat, marañuelas (conventional cookies), and cabrales cheese while sipping on a refreshing drink of Asturian cider.
- Explore Old Town's exciting nightlife after supper. There are several clubs, pubs, and cafes here that serve drinks and have live music until late in the evening. Dance the night away to contemporary beats or traditional Asturian music by joining the locals for a boisterous fiesta.

Day 2: Cultural Immersion

Morning:

- Visit the Asturias Archaeological Museum first thing in the morning to learn about the ancient history of the area through an intriguing array of relics and displays. Find out about the ancient settlements, Roman conquests, and mediaeval kingdoms that influenced Asturias' history and culture.
- Visit the adjacent Asturias Railway Museum after the museum to learn about the history of rail transportation

in the area. Explore old carriages, take a ride on vintage engines, and discover how the railway has changed over time from its beginnings in the 19th century.

In the afternoon:
- For lunch, head beyond the city limits to a rural restaurant (casa de Aldea) or typical Asturian village (aldea), where you may eat a hearty meal prepared using products that are gathered locally. Enjoy a variety of dishes such as robust stews, grilled meats, and freshly baked bread, accompanied by a glass of handmade cider.
- Return to Oviedo after lunch, and then spend the afternoon touring the state-of-the-art Centro Niemeyer, a cultural hub in the neighbouring city of Avilés. The centre was created by the well-known Brazilian architect Oscar Niemeyer, and art and architecture lovers should not miss it for its spectacular architecture and cutting-edge design.
- Experience its exhibition areas, outdoor sculptures, and cultural events to fully immerse yourself in the inventive spirit that characterises this singular cultural complex.

Evening:
- In the heart of Oviedo, have dinner at a contemporary restaurant serving creative food influenced by the flavours and customs of Asturias. Savour appetisers like grilled

octopus, creamy rice pudding, and seafood paella while sipping on a glass of regional wine or cider.

- Visit one of Oviedo's theatres or music halls for a live performance or cultural event after supper. Oviedo boasts a thriving cultural scene with a wide range of events, including concerts of classical music, modern dance performances, and experimental theatre shows.

Day 3: Outdoor Adventures

Morning:

- Get up early and take a day trip to the Picos de Europa National Park, which is close by. It's an amazing natural paradise with lots of outdoor activities and experiences. Numerous options for adventure and discovery are presented by the park's different landscapes and ecosystems, whether you're interested in hiking, mountain biking, rock climbing, or wildlife observation.
- Hike along beautiful paths in the morning, such as the Ruta del Cares or the Lagos de Covadonga, for breathtaking vistas of craggy mountains, verdant forests, and glistening lakes. Navigating the rough terrain of the park, keep a lookout for native animals including chamois, golden eagles, and wild boar.

In the afternoon:

- For lunch, have a picnic in the park or stop at a wayside cafe (chiringuito) or rustic mountain inn (refugio) to refuel with robust mountain fare. Savour regional favourites like grilled trout, baked bread, and Asturian bean stew while sipping cool mountain spring water.
- Visit one of the park's natural landmarks, such as the Covadonga Lakes, the Fuente Dé cable car, or the Cares Gorge, to continue your outdoor experience after lunch. Take in the breathtaking grandeur of these natural beauties and lose yourself in the peace of the surrounding forest.

Evening:

- Return to Oviedo as the sun is setting and treat yourself to a well-earned meal at one of the best restaurants in town. Savour a superb dining experience with inventive flavours and locally produced ingredients, accompanied by fine wine or craft beer choices.
- Take a leisurely stroll in Parque de Invierno, the largest urban park in Oviedo, after supper to decompress and rejuvenate. Savour the refreshing evening breeze, take in the sights and sounds of nature, and think back on the experiences you've had exploring Oviedo's rich past, vibrant present, and breathtaking scenery.

As we come to the end of our three-day schedule, I hope you have had fun discovering everything Oviedo has to offer. Whatever your interests—history, culture, or the great outdoors—Oviedo has a wealth of experiences just waiting to be explored. Come experience the charm of Oviedo, where there is a treasure waiting to be discovered around every corner and every minute is an exciting new adventure. Hasta luego and safe travels!

CHAPTER VII

OVIEDO'S DINING AND CUISINE

A Culinary Adventure

Welcome to Oviedo, where each meal is an innovative and traditional celebration of Asturian cuisine. We'll look at the diverse range of tastes, ingredients, and recipes that make up the regional cuisine in this section. Oviedo boasts a varied dining scene that suits all tastes, ranging from inventive fusion dishes to classic Asturian specialties. Together, let's explore the diverse food culture of the city on a culinary adventure.

7.1 Traditional Asturian Cuisine

The robust and savoury meals that highlight the region's maritime setting, agricultural past, and rocky terrain are characteristic of Asturian cuisine. Asturian cuisine is a celebration of regional products and time-honoured recipes passed down through the centuries, featuring everything from handmade cheeses and sweet delights to fresh fish and substantial stews. Here are a few foods and treats you really must sample while visiting Oviedo:

- **Fabada Asturiana:** Known as the national cuisine of Asturias, fabada asturiana is a robust bean stew consisting of pork shoulder, chorizo, white beans, and morcilla (blood sausage). Fabada asturiana is a popular dish served with crusty bread and Asturian cider on chilly winter nights. It is slow-cooked until it is soft and tasty.
- Cachopo is a filling dish consisting of breaded and fried beef or pork fillets packed with cheese and ham. It is a typical Asturian delight. A side order of fries or roasted potatoes and a crisp green salad are common accompaniments to cachopo, which is served hot and golden brown. Because of its rich flavour and pleasant texture, it's a favourite with both locals and tourists.
- **Asturian Cheeses:** The region's dairy farming heritage and verdant meadows are reflected in the wide range of artisanal cheeses produced in Asturias. Asturian cheeses are available in a variety of flavours and textures to suit every palate, ranging from mild Vidiago and nutty Gamoneu to creamy Cabrales and sour Afuega'l Pitu. To create a delectable cheese presentation that showcases the finest of Asturian dairy products, pair them with crusty bread, quince jam, or locally produced honey.
- **Seafood:** Asturias is a seafood lover's dream come true with its extensive coastline and plethora of fishing spots. Try some freshly caught seafood, including razor clams, mussels, and hake, as well as sea bass, monkfish, and clams. For a taste of the sea, don't pass up the chance to

sample Asturian specialties like shellfish stew (mariscada) or grilled octopus (pulpo a la gallega).

- **Desserts and Sweet Treats:** In Asturias, a meal wouldn't be complete without a sweet treat or two. Try regional bakeries' and pastry shops' handcrafted chocolates, pastries, and confections, or indulge in classic desserts like carbayones (almond pastries), frixuelos (Asturian crepes), and arroz con leche (rice pudding).

7.2 Recommended Restaurants and Cafes

There is a thriving food scene in Oviedo with options to suit every taste and budget. There are plenty of options to sate your culinary demands, ranging from modern cafes and inventive gastronomic concepts to classic Asturian taverns and family-run restaurants. When you're in Oviedo, check out these cafes and eateries that are suggested:

- Casa Ramón is a well-known establishment that has been providing authentic Asturian food since 1938. It is situated in the centre of Oviedo's Old Town. Casa Ramón is an excellent place to experience true Asturian cuisine, offering delicious meals like fabada asturiana, cachopo, and grilled fish, along with a welcoming atmosphere and attentive service.

- Tierra Astur is a cider house and rustic bar that showcases the finest of Asturian cuisine and culture. Tierra Astur, housed in a historic structure with a view of the busy Plaza del Fontán in Oviedo, serves a large menu of traditional Asturian fare and has an outstanding assortment of Asturian cheeses and ciders. Try their renowned cider-pouring ritual, in which servers pour cider from a height to improve its flavour and aerate it.

- **La Corte de Pelayo:** This elegant restaurant serves a contemporary take on Asturian food and is tucked away beneath Oviedo's majestic Cathedral of San Salvador. Leading chef Nacho Manzano, who has been awarded two Michelin stars for his inventive cuisine, is in charge of La Corte de Pelayo, a sophisticated restaurant that features inventive meals that highlight the finest Asturian ingredients and preparation methods.

- **El Fontán Market:** This lively marketplace in the centre of Old Town offers a taste of Oviedo's thriving culinary industry in an easygoing atmosphere. A wide variety of vendors selling prepared foods, fish, meats, cheeses, and fresh fruit can be found here, along with artisanal goods like bread, pastries, and chocolates. Have a picnic in the neighbouring San Francisco Park after grabbing a bite to eat from one of the market's many food booths.

- **Café Regina:** This is the ideal place to unwind if you're in the mood for a leisurely coffee break or breakfast. Café Regina serves light fare for breakfast and lunch and is housed in a quaint historic building with a bright outside patio. Its menu has freshly prepared coffees, teas, and artisanal pastries. Take in the atmosphere of this little neighbourhood café while you relax, enjoy a cup of coffee, and watch the world go by.

7.3 Food Festivals and Markets

Oviedo offers a range of food festivals, fairs, and culinary events all year long that highlight the finest of Asturian cuisine and culture. These events, which range from classic cider festivals to seafood celebrations to gourmet food fairs, provide guests the chance to partake in workshops, tastings, and cooking demos while also sampling a variety of regional specialties and artisanal goods. The following are some of the best food markets and festivals in Oviedo to visit:

- **Fiesta de la Sidra Natural:** Taking place in Oviedo's Old Town in late September, the Fiesta de la Sidra Natural is a vibrant celebration of Asturian cider culture. Aside from sampling a range of ciders from regional producers and witnessing traditional cider-pouring demonstrations, visitors may also take in live music, dancing performances, and Asturian specialty street food booths.
- **Feria de la Ascensión:** Celebrated each year in May, the Feria de la Ascensión is an agricultural fair that ushers in spring and the abundance of harvest season produce.

Along with live entertainment, traditional Asturian dances, fresh fruit, flowers, plants, and artisanal products from nearby farmers and artisans, visitors can peruse the stands.

- Plaza de Trascorrales in Oviedo is home to the well-known artisan and food market, Mercado de Artesanía y Alimentación, which is held on the first Sunday of each month. In addition to sampling regional cheeses, charcuterie, preserves, and baked goods from Asturian farmers and artists, guests can peruse booths offering jewellery, textiles, ceramics, and handcrafted crafts.

- **Feria del Queso de Cuerres:** Held annually in July in the nearby village of Cuerres, this cheese festival is one that cheese aficionados won't want to miss. In addition to participating in workshops, tastings, and cheese-making demonstrations conducted by local professionals, guests can enjoy an extensive assortment of artisanal cheeses from Asturias and beyond.

- **Feria de la Cocina de Asturias:** Celebrating the best of Asturian gastronomy and cuisine, the Feria de la Cocina de Asturias is a culinary fair hosted in the Exhibition and Conference Center in Oviedo. In addition to watching cooking competitions and demonstrations, visitors can sample meals from renowned chefs and restaurants and buy gourmet foods and locally produced goods from artisanal producers and sellers.

These are only a handful of the numerous food markets and festivals that Oviedo hosts all year long. Whether you're a gourmet, a food aficionado, or just interested in learning more about Asturian food and culture, these events provide a special chance to sample Oviedo's flavours and learn about Asturias' extensive culinary legacy. Come hungry, curious, and prepared to savour Oviedo's culinary marvels, where each dish is a sensory feast and each bite narrates a tale of passion, tradition, and inventiveness.

CHAPTER VIII

OVIEDO ACCOMMODATIONS

A Combination of Coziness and Charm

Every trip experience must include finding the ideal location to stay, and Oviedo has a variety of lodging choices to fit every taste, budget, and preference. After a day of taking in the city's vibrant culture and breathtaking scenery, there's no shortage of places to relax and refuel, from little guesthouses and boutique hotels to opulent resorts and historic paradores. We'll examine the different kinds of lodging in Oviedo in this area, emphasising both luxurious and affordable accommodations for visitors looking for convenience, comfort, and charm.

8.1 Types of Accommodation in Oviedo

- **Hotels:** Oviedo has a wide range of hotel alternatives, from elegant five-star facilities to more affordable options. There are many options to choose from, whether you're searching for a boutique hotel with a historic charm or a conveniently located hotel with contemporary conveniences. To ensure a pleasant and memorable stay, many hotels in Oviedo provide amenities like free Wi-Fi, breakfast, and concierge services.

- **Guesthouses and Bed & Breakfasts: If** you're looking for a more secluded and customised stay in Oviedo, think about booking a room at one of these establishments. These quaint lodging options, which are frequently owned by families, provide a friendly environment where visitors can feel like members of the family. When visiting Oviedo, take advantage of the home-cooked breakfasts, insider advice from hospitable hosts, and a cosy place to stay.

- **Apartments and Vacation Rentals:** Those looking for freedom and flexibility while visiting Oviedo may choose to stay in an apartment or rent a vacation home. All the conveniences of home are available in these self-catering units, including fully functional kitchens, living spaces, and private bathrooms. Apartments and holiday rentals are great for families, parties, and extended visits since they provide you the flexibility to see Oviedo at your speed and still have the conveniences of a private home.

- **Hostels:** Oviedo's hostels offer a wide range of reasonably priced lodging options for those on a tight budget. In addition to private rooms for those wishing a little more privacy, hostels also provide shared bathroom facilities in the form of dormitories. Hostels are a terrific way to meet other travellers and make new friends while visiting Oviedo on a budget, especially since they often have shared kitchens, social rooms, and organised events like walking tours and bar crawls.

- **Paradores:** Located in Oviedo and other parts of Spain, paradores are state-run hotels that offer a genuinely unique and unforgettable experience. These repurposed palaces, monasteries, and castles offer opulent lodging in gorgeous settings while fusing contemporary conveniences with historic charm dating back centuries. Indulge in opulence, history, and culture in an Oviedo Parador, where each visit is an adventure through time.

8.2 Budget-Friendly Options

- **Hostal Arcos:** This accessible, reasonably priced lodging option is situated in the centre of Oviedo's Old Town. Basic facilities including free Wi-Fi, flat-screen TVs, and private bathrooms are provided in the tidy and comfortable rooms. Take advantage of the hostel's prime location to walk around Oviedo's attractions and enjoy free coffee and tea in the common room.

- **Pensión Romero:** Conveniently located next to Oviedo's train station, Pensión Romero is an inexpensive guesthouse that provides guests on a tight budget with basic yet cosy lodging. Cosy and immaculate rooms with shared bathrooms, heating, and free WiFi are available. The welcoming staff of the guesthouse is pleased to offer suggestions for dining establishments, points of interest, and recreational pursuits to enable visitors to make the most of their time in Oviedo.

- **Albergue Turístico La Peregrina:** This centrally located hostel offers inexpensive dormitory-style lodgings, making it ideal for tourists on a tight budget. The hostel has an outside terrace, living room, and community kitchen where visitors may unwind and mingle with other backpackers. Travellers looking for reasonably priced lodging in Oviedo frequently choose Albergue Turístico La Peregrina because of its welcoming atmosphere and practical features.

8.3 Luxury Stays

- **Hotel de la Reconquista:** This five-star luxury hotel in the centre of Oviedo is housed in a landmark 18th-century edifice and provides elegance, comfort, and flawless service. With exquisitely furnished rooms and suites, fine dining options, and opulent facilities like an indoor swimming pool, fitness centre, and spa, Hotel de la Reconquista is the ideal choice for discerning visitors looking for an unforgettable and opulent stay in Oviedo.
- Luxurious refuge offering peace, relaxation, and renewal is the Gran Hotel Las Caldas Wellness Clinic, which is tucked away in the verdant countryside not far from

Oviedo. The hotel, which is surrounded by lovely gardens and natural hot springs, has expansive rooms and suites with panoramic views in addition to a top-notch spa and wellness area that provides a variety of therapies and treatments meant to enhance health and wellbeing.

- **Eurostars Hotel de la Reconquista:** Another opulent choice in Oviedo, this hotel creates an incredibly memorable experience by fusing modern luxury with ancient charm. Situated in the centre of the city, within a tastefully renovated 18th-century palace, the hotel boasts sophisticated guestrooms and suites, fine dining options, and exclusive features including a fitness centre, rooftop terrace, and concierge services. Oviedo's ultimate luxury establishment is the Eurostars Hotel de la Reconquista, which exudes unmatched elegance and sophistication.

Oviedo has a variety of lodging options to meet the needs and tastes of any traveller, whether they are looking for lavish stays or affordable lodging. Throughout your trip to this enchanting city, you'll discover the ideal location to unwind and rejuvenate, ranging from quaint guesthouses and boutique hotels to five-star resorts and historic paradores. Prepare to discover the charm of Oviedo, where charm meets comfort and every visit is an adventure just waiting to be experienced, by packing your bags, making hotel reservations, and getting set to explore.

CHAPTER IX

SHOPPING IN OVIEDO

Discovering Treasures and Local Delights

Oviedo offers a fantastic shopping experience that combines trendy boutiques, lively marketplaces, and traditional craftsmanship. Oviedo offers something for every kind of shopper, whether you're looking for unusual mementos to remember your vacation or just want to indulge in a little retail therapy. This section will cover the city's thriving retail environment, which includes everything from crowded markets and shopping districts to little boutiques and artisanal businesses.

9.1 Souvenirs and Local Products

Oviedo offers a wide selection of locally made goods and souvenirs that are a reflection of the region's artisanal traditions and cultural legacy. A plethora of treasures await you to explore and bring home as keepsakes of your visit to Oviedo, ranging from superb wines and gourmet delights to traditional textiles and crafts. The following are some of the best keepsakes and regional goods to search for:

- **Asturian Cider:** Without trying the famed sidra, or cider, from the area, a trip to Oviedo isn't complete. Asturian cider is a renowned centuries-old tradition in Asturias, made from apples picked locally and aged in traditional wooden barrels. Grab a bottle of cider to sip throughout your vacation, or stop by a neighbourhood cider house (sidrería) to try a range of ciders and discover how they're made.
- **Cheeses from Asturias:** Asturias is well known for its handcrafted cheeses, which have a wide range of tastes, textures, and designs. There is a cheese to suit every palate, ranging from acidic cow's milk cheeses like Gamoneu to velvety blue cheeses like Cabrales. To sample and buy a variety of Asturian cheeses to savour during your visit or to bring home as gifts for friends and family, stop by a nearby cheese market or store.
- **Asturian Crafts:** Oviedo is home to a thriving community of woodworkers, potters, and other artisans who create a vast array of handcrafted products, textiles, and ceramics. Discover handcrafted gifts like finely woven tapestries, hand-carved wooden objects, and handmade pottery by exploring the city's artisanal shops and craft fairs. These unique items are ideal mementos to reminisce about your stay in Oviedo.
- **Asturian Gastronomy:** Treat your palate to a variety of regional gastronomy specialties and delights, and bring a taste of Asturias home with you. Delectable options are

abundant, ranging from traditional sweets like Asturian honey, chestnut honey, and artisanal chocolates to savoury goodies like Asturian sausages (embutidos) and canned seafood (conservas). Stock up on these delectables at your neighbourhood specialty food store or gourmet shop so you can prepare an Asturian-inspired feast at home.

9.2 Shopping Districts and Markets

There are several different markets, retail centres, and boutiques in Oviedo where you may go window shopping and buy until you drop. There is something for every kind of shopper to enjoy, from contemporary shopping malls and lively markets to charming lanes dotted with craft stores. The following are some of Oviedo's best marketplaces and retail areas to visit:

- **Calle Uría:** Known as the major shopping route in Oviedo, Calle Uría is a busy avenue with a mix of department stores, high-end boutiques, and foreign brands. Enjoy a trip down Calle Uría to peruse the newest styles, purchase designer labels, and get mementos and presents for loved ones back home.

- **Mercado El Fontán:** This ancient covered market, which has been around since the sixteenth century, is situated in the centre of Oviedo's Old Town. Numerous vendors offering local goods, meats, cheeses, seafood, and fresh veggies may be found here. While you browse the market's meandering aisles for fresh produce and upscale goods, taste the flavours of Asturias.

- **Plaza del Fontán:** Located next to the Mercado El Fontán, this bustling square comes to life on market days with street sellers, craftspeople, and entertainers. As you visit this lively outdoor market, look through stalls selling jewellery, apparel, souvenirs, and handcrafted crafts while taking in the festive ambiance.

- **Príncipe Felipe Street:** Known for its blend of high-end boutiques, specialty stores, and global brands, Príncipe Felipe Street is a well-liked shopping destination in Oviedo. Explore shops that offer clothing, home products, accessories, and more as you stroll down the road surrounded by trees. As you browse and explore, take a break for a bite or coffee at one of the quaint cafés along the street to observe the passing scene.

- **Shopping Centers:** Oviedo is home to several contemporary malls and shopping centres with a variety of stores, eateries, and entertainment venues housed under one roof. For an exciting day of shopping and entertainment, visit stores like Intu Asturias or Centro Comercial Salesas to purchase apparel, electronics, home items, and more. You can also take advantage of the restaurants, movie theatres, and kid-friendly play areas.

Oviedo has a bustling and varied retail scene that suits every taste and budget, whether you're looking for one-of-a-kind souvenirs, gourmet treats, or the newest fashion trends. So gather your shopping essentials and get set to visit the city's quaint shops, vibrant marketplaces, and cutting-edge retail areas, where each acquisition is a hidden gem just waiting to be found.

CHAPTER X

OVIEDO NIGHTLIFE AND ENTERTAINMENT

Where the City Comes Alive

When the sun sets on Oviedo's charming streets, the city comes alive with activity and entertainment. Oviedo has a wide range of options to fit every taste and mood, from elegant taverns and cosy bars to exciting theatrical productions and vibrant music venues. This section delves into the vibrant nightlife of the city, showcasing the top clubs, pubs, theatres, and live music venues where you can soak up the excitement and energy of Oviedo after dark.

10.1 Pubs and Bars

- **El Último Trago:** Nestled in a quaint alleyway in Oviedo's Old Town, this quaint tavern is well-known for its welcoming ambiance and helpful staff. Enter and grab a seat at the bar to savour a menu of tapas and small dishes cooked with fresh, locally sourced ingredients, as well as a variety of creative cocktails, exquisite wines, and local beers. El Último Trago's colourful décor and laid-back atmosphere make it the ideal place to relax and have a long drink with friends.

- **La Ley Seca:** Known for its vibrant ambiance and varied programming, La Ley Seca is a well-liked bar and live music venue located in the centre of Oviedo's old quarter. Regular live music events at the pub feature local bands and performers performing a variety of genres, such as Latin, jazz, blues, and rock. At La Ley Seca, every night is a celebration of music and culture. Grab a drink, hit the dance floor, and let the music take you away.

- **El Café de las Artes:** Located in the cultural district of Oviedo, nestled in a historic building, this young and stylish café-bar draws a varied clientele of both locals and tourists. The bar's diverse décor, which includes modern artwork, exposed brick walls, and old furniture, creates a special and welcoming atmosphere. Savour a menu of light appetisers and snacks along with a variety of craft beers, specialty cocktails, and gourmet coffee drinks. El Café de las Artes, with its laid-back vibe and artistic flair, is the ideal place to mingle, unwind, and spend a night on the town in Oviedo.

- Don't miss La Galería de los Vinos, a quaint wine bar situated in the centre of Oviedo's wine area, if you're a wine enthusiast. In addition to a wide range of wines from Spain and around the globe, the bar serves a menu of tapas and small plates that are meant to go well with the wines. La Galería de los Vinos, housed in a historic structure featuring stone walls and vaulted ceilings, embodies an air of refinement and old-world charm, making it the ideal location for a small-scale get-together with friends or a romantic evening.

10.2 Live Music Venues

- One of Oviedo's best live music venues, Sala Acapulco is housed in the historic Teatro Campoamor's basement and often hosts concerts and shows by both local and foreign performers. The location has a large dance floor, cosy sitting sections, and cutting-edge lighting and sound systems. Sala Acapulco has an eclectic array of performers and events to fit every musical taste, ranging from pop and rock to techno and independent music.

- Teatro de la Laboral is a renowned theatre and performance space that holds a variety of cultural events, such as theatrical shows, dance performances, concerts, and more. Teatro de la Laboral is located amid the expansive grounds of the Laboral Ciudad de la Cultura. Oviedo's premier location for live entertainment is Teatro de la Laboral, which boasts state-of-the-art acoustics, a movable stage, and modern facilities.

- One of Oviedo's most recognizable features, Teatro Campoamor is the site of numerous other cultural events and performances all year long in addition to the city's well-known opera festival. Teatro Campoamor has a varied and captivating schedule of events that highlight the finest of Oviedo's cultural landscape, ranging from cinema screenings and theatrical productions to classical music concerts and ballet performances.

- The popular nightclub and live music venue La Salvaje is situated in the centre of Oviedo's nightlife zone. The club attracts large numbers of partygoers eager to dance the night away to the newest songs and hottest tracks because of its large dance floor, cutting-edge sound system, and lively environment. La Salvaje, with its vibrant atmosphere and upbeat feel, is the best place to go for entertainment and nightlife in Oviedo.

10.3 Performances and Theater

- **Teatro Filarmónica:** The lovely Teatro Filarmónica is located in the centre of Oviedo and is housed in a historic building. It presents a wide range of productions, such as plays, musicals, dance acts, and more. The compact setting, elaborate décor, and superb acoustics of Teatro Filarmónica provide an immersive and distinctive theatrical experience that carries viewers to a different realm.

- Escenario Uno is a modern theatre and performance space that features avant-garde performances and experimental works by both local and foreign artists. It is situated in the lively La Ería district. Escenario Uno provides a dynamic and avant-garde approach to theatre and performance art in Oviedo, ranging from interactive installations and immersive experiences to avant-garde theatre and multimedia performances.

- **Centro Niemeyer:** Designed by renowned Brazilian architect Oscar Niemeyer, Centro Niemeyer is a contemporary cultural complex located in the neighbouring city of Avilés. A vast array of cultural events and performances are held at the centre, such as concerts, theatrical plays, movie screenings, and art exhibits. For visitors to Oviedo and the surrounding area, Centro Niemeyer offers a singular and unforgettable cultural experience with its spectacular architecture, cutting-edge amenities, and varied program of activities.

- **Teatro Jovellanos:** A 19th-century historic theatre and performance space, Teatro Jovellanos is situated in the neighbouring city of Gijón. The theatre presents a wide range of artistic events and performances, such as dance performances, music concerts, theatre productions, and more. Theatre aficionados and cultural vultures in Oviedo and beyond should not miss Teatro Jovellanos because of its exquisite building, cosy setting, and top-notch programming.

Oviedo has a lively and varied nightlife and entertainment scene that appeals to every taste and interest, whether you're looking to relax with a drink at a little bar, dance the night away at a live music venue, or immerse yourself in the arts at a theatre play. Put on your dancing shoes, purchase your tickets, and get ready to explore Oviedo's nightlife, which promises to be exciting and energetic.

CHAPTER XI

PRACTICAL INFORMATION

To guarantee a seamless and pleasurable trip, you must acquaint yourself with some useful facts before leaving for Oviedo. Being prepared can make your vacation to this enchanting city more enjoyable. This includes knowing the local currency and payment options, learning some basic communication skills, and honouring customs and decorum. We'll go over all you need to know in this part to travel Oviedo like a pro.

11.1 Currency and Payment Methods

When visiting Oviedo, it's a good idea to have some cash on hand for small purchases and transactions, especially in markets, cafes, and smaller places that might not accept credit or debit cards. The official currency of Spain is the Euro (€), represented by the symbol "EUR." Nonetheless, the majority of major credit and debit cards, including American Express, Mastercard, and Visa, are generally accepted in the city's hotels, eateries, and retail establishments. In Oviedo, ATMs are widely dispersed and enable you to take out cash using your debit or credit card as needed. Before leaving, it's a good idea to let your bank know about your trip plans to make sure your cards will function overseas and to find out if there will be any additional fees for foreign transactions or currency conversion.

11.2 Language and Communication Tips

Spanish (Castilian) is the official language of Oviedo and all of Spain. Even while many Oviedo locals, particularly in tourist areas and establishments, may know a little English, it's still beneficial to acquire a few fundamental Spanish expressions and phrases to improve communication and your interactions with locals. To get you going, consider these key phrases:

- **Hola:** Hello
- **Gracias:** Thank you
- **Por favor:** Please
- **¿Dónde está...?:** Where is...?
- **La cuenta, por favor:** The check, please
- **¿Cuánto cuesta?:** How much does it cost?
- **Sí:** Yes
- **No:** No

Respecting and appreciating the local way of life can be demonstrated by attempting to say "Hola" to locals and "Gracias" or "Por favor" when it's suitable. Additionally, you may ensure smooth communication during your stay in Oviedo by utilising basic gestures like nodding or pointing to help overcome any language issues.

11.3 Local Customs and Etiquette

It's important to observe regional etiquette and customs when visiting Oviedo to respect the area's culture and traditions. The following are important traditions and manners to bear in mind:

- **Salutations:** Salutations play a significant role in social interactions in Spain. It is usual to say "Hola" (hello) , shake hands with people you meet for the first time, or kiss someone on the cheek if you are an acquaintance. When extending a warm greeting to people, don't forget to smile and maintain eye contact.

- **Mealtimes:** In general, Spanish people eat supper (la cena) between 8:30 and 10:30 pm and lunch (la comida) between 1:30 and 3:30 pm. Particularly in smaller towns and villages, eateries in Oviedo typically close for a siesta (midday nap) between 3:30 and 8:30 p.m. When dining out, it's normal to linger over meals and enjoy leisurely conversation with dining partners. It's also polite to wait until everyone at the table has been served before starting to eat.

- **Tipping:** Although it's not as customary or expected in Spain as it is in some other nations, it's always appreciated for very good service. If you are pleased with the service at a restaurant, it is traditional to offer a little tip of roughly 5–10% of the entire bill. But tipping is not required, so if the service is poor, you don't have to feel pressured to leave a tip.

- **Respecting Personal Space:** Unlike you may be used to, Spaniards cherish personal space and may stand closer to one another during chats. It's critical to respect people's personal space and refrain from approaching too closely or making physical contact with them unless invited. Furthermore, pay attention to noise levels and refrain from talking loudly or creating a commotion in public settings, particularly late at night or in residential areas.

By keeping in mind these traditions and manners, you'll show respect for Oviedo's local way of life and guarantee pleasant encounters with residents while you're there.

In summary

Now that you have this useful knowledge, you may confidently and easily traverse Oviedo. You'll be able to thoroughly immerse yourself in the rich culture and traditions of this fascinating city by learning about the local currency, how to pay with it, how to communicate effectively, and how to observe local customs and etiquette. So prepare for an incredible journey in Oviedo, where there is always something new and fascinating to explore. Pack your luggage, brush up on those Spanish words, and get set. ¡Happy travels!

CHAPTER 12

OVIEDO TRANSPORTATION

Your Start Point for Discovery

It can seem impossible at times to navigate a new city, but worry not! Oviedo's well-functioning transit infrastructure and easy access to neighbouring attractions make travelling about the city a snap. Oviedo has everything you need, whether you're travelling from a distance, taking day trips, or exploring the city. We'll cover all you need to know to travel comfortably and confidently in and around this quaint city in our in-depth guide to transportation.

12.1 Getting to Oviedo

- **By Air:** Asturias Airport (OVD), which is about 47 kilometres northwest of the city centre, is the closest airport to Oviedo. The airport offers connectivity to important locations in Spain and Europe for both local and international flights. There are several ways to go from the airport to Oviedo: taxis, public buses, airport shuttles, and rental automobiles. Asturias Airport is a convenient and easily accessible entry point into Oviedo, taking about 30 to 40 minutes to get there by vehicle or shuttle.

- **By Train:** Renfe operates regular train services that connect Oviedo to the Spanish rail network. Oviedo Railway Station (Estación de Oviedo), the city's principal train station, is conveniently accessible from various regions of Spain due to its central location. In addition to long-distance and regional services to locations including Santiago de Compostela, Madrid, Barcelona, and Bilbao, Renfe provides high-speed AVE trains. Train tickets can be bought online, at the station, or through third-party booking platforms. Depending on personal tastes and financial constraints, passengers can select from a variety of pricing classes and seat choices.

- **By Bus:** Several bus companies provide long-distance and regional bus services from Oviedo to locations across Spain and beyond. Oviedo Bus Station (Estación de Autobuses de Oviedo), the city's principal bus terminal, is situated close to the city centre and provides connections to Asturias' major cities and villages as well as surrounding areas including Cantabria, Galicia, and Castilla y León. One of the major bus companies that serves Oviedo is ALSA, which offers services that go to places like Gijón, Avilés, León, and Madrid. Bus tickets can be bought online, at the station, or from licensed ticket sellers. There are options for one-way or round-trip tickets, as well as various seating configurations to suit different tastes and price ranges.

12.2 How to Navigate Oviedo

- **Public Transportation:** Public transportation is provided by Empresa Municipal de Transportes Urbanos de Oviedo (EMTUSA), which runs a thorough network of buses and trams across the city. With multiple routes covering neighbourhoods, suburbs, and outlying areas, the city's bus network is extensive. When boarding the bus, passengers can buy single-ride or multi-journey passes from ticket machines, authorised dealers, or the driver directly. Furthermore, Oviedo's tram system, Tranvía de Oviedo, offers quick and environmentally friendly ways to move around the city centre and link to important sites and attractions. Tram tickets can be bought using cash or contactless payment methods from ticket machines at tram stops or while riding the tram.

- **Taxi:** Taxis are a practical and adaptable form of transportation that is widely accessible around Oviedo. Taxis can be requested in advance over the phone or by mobile apps, or they can be hailed on the street. The local government sets the fare rates, which usually include a base fare plus additional fees determined by the distance travelled and the amount of time spent in the taxi. When the trip is over, passengers should make sure the taxi metre is running and ask for a printed receipt. It is simple to locate a taxi when needed because taxi stands are positioned at strategic locations across the city, such as tourist attractions, busy intersections, and hubs for transportation.

- **Bicycle:** Riding a bike is a convenient and pleasurable way to explore Oviedo, as the city has designated bike lanes and trails. There are several rental shops and bike-sharing programs in Oviedo where visitors can pick up and drop off bicycles for an hour, a day, or a week. Riding a bicycle lets you easily negotiate Oviedo's narrow streets and alleyways, explore the city at your speed, and find off-the-beaten-path hidden gems and local treasures. Just keep in mind to wear a helmet, obey traffic laws, and lock your bike safely while not in use to guard against damage or theft.

12.3 Day Trips and Excursions

- **Gijón:** Gijón is a bustling coastal city that is only 30 kilometres northwest of Oviedo. It is renowned for its stunning beaches, varied cultural offerings, and energetic environment. Gijón is easily reached from Oviedo by rail or bus. Visitors can spend the day exploring the city's quaint Old Town, meandering along the waterfront promenade, and savouring fresh seafood at one of the many eateries and cafes that have a view of the sea.

- **Covadonga:** Famous for both its breathtaking natural beauty and historical significance, Covadonga is a charming mountain community tucked away amid the Picos de Europa National Park. From Oviedo, visitors can take a picturesque drive or take a guided tour to Covadonga, where they can see famous sites like the Sanctuary of Covadonga, the Holy Cave (Cueva Santa), and the breathtaking Lakes of Covadonga (Lagos de Covadonga), which provide breath-taking views of the surrounding valleys and mountains.

- **Avilés:** A picturesque mediaeval town with a rich history and cultural legacy, Avilés is located about 25 kilometres northeast of Oviedo. From Oviedo, travellers may take a quick train or bus ride to Avilés, where they can tour the city's well-preserved mediaeval centre, stop at famous locations like the Church of San Nicolás and the Palacio de Camposagrado, and take in the vibrant arts and cultural scene that includes theatres, galleries, and museums.

- **Cudillero:** Known for its vibrant homes, meandering alleyways, and busy harbour, Cudillero is a charming fishing community perched on cliffs overlooking the Cantabrian Sea. From Oviedo, visitors may enjoy a scenic car or bus journey to Cudillero, where they can spend the day strolling around the quaint streets, dining at local eateries serving fresh seafood, and taking in the breath-blowing views of the coast.

Oviedo is a great place to start exploring the beauty and diversity of Asturias and beyond because of its easy access to many sights and locations, as well as its efficient transit options. Oviedo provides several chances for exploration and adventure, whether you're travelling by bus, rail, or aeroplane, taking public transportation to get around the city, or taking day trips to explore neighbouring cities and sites. Prepare for an amazing adventure to the heart of northern Spain by packing your baggage and making your schedule.

CHAPTER 13

HEALTH AND SAFETY GUIDE

Ensuring Your Well-Being in Oviedo

Travelling through Oviedo is a fascinating adventure, but it's important to put your health and safety first to make the trip worry-free. Being ready and knowledgeable is essential whether you're exploring the great outdoors, enjoying local food, or taking in historical sites. We'll go over everything you should know to be safe and healthy while visiting Oviedo in our in-depth guide on health and safety.

13.1 Contacts for Emergencies

- **Emergency Services:** To contact emergency services in Spain, including police, fire, and medical aid, dial 112, which is the country's universal emergency number. The operators will quickly send out the proper response teams to help you, as they are trained to handle a variety of circumstances.

- **Police:** You can get in touch with the neighbourhood police station for non-emergency circumstances, missing property help, reporting small occurrences, or information requests. Policia Nacional (National Police) phone number 091, Policia Local (Local Police) phone number 092. These services are ready to help you with any issues you may have while visiting Oviedo, and they run around the clock.

- **Embassy or Consulate:** It's important to keep your nation's embassy or consulate's contact details close at hand in case you need assistance from them when travelling abroad. Your embassy or consulate can offer assistance in cases of lost or stolen documents, medical emergencies, or other pressing issues. Make sure you have their addresses and phone numbers in a secure location so you can readily access them.

13.2 Medical Facilities

- **Hospitals and Clinics:** Oviedo has up-to-date healthcare centres and hospitals that can manage a variety of illnesses and medical crises. One of Oviedo's primary hospitals, Hospital Universitario Central de Asturias (HUCA), offers a wide range of medical services, including emergency care and specialty therapies. Apart from that, you can get regular check-ups and non-emergency medical care at any of the city's many clinics and health facilities.

- **Pharmacies:** Known as "farmacias" in Spanish, pharmacies are widely distributed around Oviedo and provide a large assortment of prescription drugs, over-the-counter medications, and health-related items. Professionals with extensive training and pharmacists can offer guidance on mild illnesses, suggest appropriate drugs, and help with medical questions. Pharmacies can be found by looking for the green cross that is usually posted outside of them. You should also confirm their hours of operation, as they might differ.

- **Medical Insurance:** It's crucial to be sure you have sufficient coverage for unforeseen illnesses, accidents, or emergencies before coming to Oviedo. Make sure your insurance covers all of the following: hospital stays, emergency medical evacuation, repatriation, and medical costs. Consider getting travel insurance made especially for overseas travel if your present insurance plan doesn't give enough coverage. It can offer extra benefits and peace of mind while you're away.

13.3 Travel Insurance

- **Coverage:** Travel insurance provides defence against a variety of unanticipated mishaps and crises that could arise while travelling, such as flight delays, lost or stolen luggage, medical crises, and personal responsibility. Make sure the travel insurance policy you choose fits your needs and offers sufficient protection for your trip to Oviedo by carefully examining the coverage limits, exclusions, and perks.

- **Medical Coverage:** Having adequate medical coverage is crucial because medical costs can quickly mount up in the event of an illness or injury when travelling overseas. Seek out a travel insurance plan that provides coverage for emergency medical evacuation, medical bills, and repatriation to your nation of origin in the event of a catastrophic illness or injury. Check if the coverage limitations match or surpass the estimated expenses of Oviedo hospital stays and medical care.

- **Cancellation and Interruption:** Several circumstances, including illness, family situations, or natural catastrophes, may cause last-minute changes to travel arrangements. Consider getting travel insurance that covers trip cancellation, trip interruption, and trip delay to guard against monetary losses brought on by these events. If your trip is disturbed or cancelled for covered causes, this coverage can compensate you for prepaid and non-refundable charges such as flights, lodging, tours, and activities.

- **24/7 Support:** Travel insurance frequently includes 24/7 emergency help services that offer round-the-clock support and assistance throughout your vacation, in addition to financial protection. A multilingual emergency hotline, medical referrals, help with misplaced or stolen documents, and emergency medical care coordination are a few examples of these services. Having access to these services can guarantee that you get the help you require when you need it most by providing priceless support and direction in trying circumstances.

In summary

You may have peace of mind and concentrate on creating treasured moments during your stay in Oviedo by putting your health and safety first and being proactive in planning ahead. To guard against unforeseen circumstances, keep emergency contacts close at hand, become acquainted with the medical services in the area, and make sure you have sufficient travel insurance. Your trip to Oviedo will be safe and rewarding, full of adventure, discovery, and life-long memories, provided you plan and prepare thoroughly. Happy travels!

CHAPTER 14

USEFUL PHRASES

Knowing a few essential phrases in Spanish before you travel to Oviedo will improve your trip and make it easier to communicate with locals. Gaining confidence and ease in traversing the city can be achieved by learning five crucial phrases, which are useful whether you're dining at a local restaurant, navigating the busy markets, or asking for help in an emergency. To make sure you're ready for everything during your trip to Oviedo, we'll go over basic Spanish phrases, dining and shopping phrases, and emergency phrases in this book.

14.1 Simple Spanish Expressions

i. Greetings and Polite Expressions:

- **Hola:** Hello
- **Buenos días:** Good morning
- **Buenas tardes:** Good afternoon
- **Buenas noches:** Good evening/night
- **Por favor:** Please
- **Gracias:** Thank you
- **De nada:** You're welcome

- **Perdón:** Excuse me/pardon me

ii. Introductions and Socialising:

- **¿Cómo te llamas?:** What's your name?
- **Me llamo...:** My name is...
- **Mucho gusto:** Nice to meet you
- **¿Cómo estás?:** How are you?
- **Estoy bien, gracias:** I'm fine, thank you
- **¿Hablas inglés?:** Do you speak English?
- **Sí, un poco:** Yes, a little bit
- **No entiendo:** I don't understand

iii. Directions and Navigation:

- **¿Dónde está...?:** Where is...?
- **¿Cómo llego a...?:** How do I get to...?
- **A la derecha:** To the right
- **A la izquierda:** To the left
- **Recto:** Straight ahead
- **Aquí:** Here
- **Allí:** There
- **¿Cuánto cuesta?:** How much does it cost?

14.2 Dining and Shopping Phrases

i. Dining Out:

- **¿Tienes una mesa libre?:** Do you have a free table?
- **La carta, por favor:** The menu, please
- **Quisiera...:** I would like...
- **Para mí...:** For me...
- **¿Qué recomiendas?:** What do you recommend?
- **La cuenta, por favor:** The bill, please
- **¿Se incluye el servicio?:** Is the tip included?

ii. Shopping:

- **¿Cuánto cuesta?:** How much does it cost?
- **¿Tienes esto en otra talla/color?:** Do you have this in another size/colour?
- **Me lo llevo:** I'll take it
- **¿Aceptan tarjeta de crédito?:** Do you accept credit cards?
- **¿Puedo pagar en efectivo?:** Can I pay in cash?
- **¿Dónde están los probadores?:** Where are the fitting rooms?
- **¿Tienen descuentos?:** Do you have any discounts?

14.3 Emergency Phrases

i. Medical Emergencies:

- **¡Ayuda!:** Help!
- **¡Llama a una ambulancia!:** Call an ambulance!
- **Necesito un médico:** I need a doctor
- **Me siento mal:** I feel unwell
- **Tengo dolor de...:** I have pain in...
- **¿Dónde está el hospital más cercano?:** Where is the nearest hospital?

ii. Lost or Stolen Items:

- **¡Mi bolso/cartera ha sido robado!:** My bag/wallet has been stolen!
- **¿Puedes ayudarme a encontrar mi...?:** Can you help me find my...?
- **Necesito reportar un robo/perdida:** I need to report a theft/loss
- **¿Dónde está la comisaría de policía más cercana?:** Where is the nearest police station?

iii. General Emergencies:

- **¡Fuego!:** Fire!
- **¡Llama a la policía!:** Call the police!
- **¡Alguien necesita ayuda!:** Someone needs help!
- **¡Detente!:** Stop!
- **¡Cuidado!:** Watch out!

When you become familiar with these helpful expressions, you'll be able to converse with locals in Oviedo with confidence and handle a variety of scenarios. To ensure proper communication, practice pronouncing words correctly and using gestures when needed. Additionally, don't be afraid to ask for clarification or assistance when you need it. A little planning and effort will help you get the most out of your trip to Oviedo and develop wonderful memories in this charming city. ¡Felicidades! (Best of luck!)

CHAPTER 15

CONCLUDING REMARKS

Your Memorable Adventure in Oviedo

It's time to take stock of the memories you've made, the moments you've treasured, and the beauty you've found in this alluring city as your trip to Oviedo draws to an end. You will surely never forget Oviedo because of everything you experienced there, including touring historical sites, enjoying delectable food, and getting fully immersed in the way of life. I'll close by giving you some last advice on how to make the most of your stay in Oviedo and then wish you a happy departure to continue your travels.

15.1 Final Tips and Recommendations

- **Immerse Yourself in the Culture:** Allow yourself to become fully immersed in Oviedo's rich cultural heritage. To learn more about the history and culture of the city, check out the museums and galleries, attend local festivals, and talk to the people who live there. You'll have a greater understanding of this fascinating place if you accept the kindness and friendliness of the Asturian people.

- **Explore Outside the City Limits:** Although Oviedo has a lot to offer inside its boundaries, don't be afraid to leave the city and explore the surrounding area. Take day trips to neighbouring cities and sites like Gijón, Covadonga, and Cudillero to see the varied scenery, quaint towns, and undiscovered treasures that Asturias has to offer.
- **Savour the Flavours of Asturian Cuisine:** The cuisine of Asturia is well-known for its robust flavours, use of seasonal products, and cooking customs. Don't forget to try the regional specialties in neighbourhood eateries and traditional sidrerías (cider houses), like fabada asturiana (bean stew), cachopo (breaded veal or pork), and sidra (Asturian cider). For a sweet finish to your meal, don't forget to savour delectable sweets like rice pudding or frixuelos, which are Asturian pancakes.
- **Keep Yourself Safe and Healthy:** Put your health and safety first when visiting Oviedo. Use sunscreen, drink plenty of water, and abide by any local health restrictions. To ensure peace of mind during your journey, carry emergency contacts and critical medical information with you. You should also think about getting travel insurance. To protect yourself and others, always remember to maintain proper hygiene and abide by any COVID-19 guidelines that may be in effect.
- **Preserve Memories:** Don't forget to preserve your memories of Oviedo by taking pictures, keeping a

journal, or buying mementos. These moments, which might include a memorable sunset over the city skyline, an intimate moment with locals, or a taste of real Asturian food, will bring back fond recollections of your amazing trip to Oviedo for years to come.

15.2 Goodbye, Oviedo

Take a minute to say goodbye to this quaint city and everything it has to offer as your stay in Oviedo comes to an end. Take the memories of your experiences in Oviedo, the warmth of Asturian hospitality, and the splendour of its surroundings with you, whether you're heading back home or continuing your journey. As you go, remember that Oviedo will always be waiting to welcome you back with open arms and be happy to share its secrets and riches. Until our next meeting, Oviedo, hasta luego! (Until then, Oviedo!)

Printed in Great Britain
by Amazon

46159214R00056